The Year of Hats

*A new collection of hats designed by the
Block Island Knitwear Collective*

Proceeds from the sale of this book will be donated to The Nature Conservancy
to support the Block Island Bird-Banding Station.

The designers in the North Light Fibers classroom. Front row (left to right): Maureen Cullen, Lynn Murphy, Kitty Savel, Amy Snell, Brenda Hyland-Miller. Back row (left to right): Katherine Gardner, Diane Tessaglia-Hymes, Jennifer Walsh, Deb Frazier, Teema Loeffelholz, Lauren Altieri, Barbara Hyland-Hill, Deborah Newton. Photo by Sven Risom, May 2023.
Cover photo by Deborah Newton.

First edition, August 2024
ISBN: 9798332279188

Book and cover design by Diane Tessaglia-Hymes, DIANETH.com

Unless otherwise credited, photos for each pattern © 2024 by that pattern's designer.

Contents

Acknowledgments

©Deborah Newton

Our sincere thanks go to Sven and Laura Risom and Karyn Logan from North Light Fibers, who inspired us with energy, beautiful yarns, and their love for Block Island.

Thanks also to the 1661 Inn on Block Island for making us welcome as a group, year after year.

Special thanks to the generous and hard-working Diane Tessaglia-Hymes for volunteering to design and organize this collection of patterns.

Proceeds from this joint project will go to support The Nature Conservancy on Block Island.

Note that each designer has lent her design for this e-book *The Year of Hats* until August 31, 2025. Beginning September 1, 2025, each hat pattern will be available according to each designer's choice—on her own website or Ravelry page, through direct contact, or not at all.

Laura and Sven Risom, our good friends and owners of North Light Fibers.

©Diane Tessaglia-Hymes

The 1661 Inn on Block Island at night.

A message from Deborah

I started teaching Knitwear Design a decade ago on beautiful Block Island, Rhode Island, home of North Light Fibers. I was generously encouraged to do this by my friends Sven and Laura Risom, owners of North Light Fibers, who spent more than a decade making unique and beautiful yarns there. The first year seemed to be a warning of sorts—we endured a hurricane—but we still had fun in our quest to better understand the elements that go into designing knitwear! After the big storm I thought, no one would ever want to come again! But that first group continues to return year after year.

A few years later, by popular demand, I started a new knitwear design group, whose inspired work you see here in this collection. The members of our small group, the Block Island Knitwear Collective, came to the little island off the Rhode Island coast from far and wide: from nearby New England, from the American south and far west, and even from distant Australia! Not only do we think seriously about knitwear, we have shared the pleasures of nature walks, bird-banding during migration time, and visits to the famous Block Island Southeast Lighthouse (see page 53).

The wonderful group has thrived, returning every spring to pursue new topics. They have enjoyed designing knitted sweaters and accessories, swatching pattern stitches, inspiring each other, and making new friends. During the rest of the year, we compare notes regularly on Zoom.

In 2023, this wonderful group made the decision to create a collection of hats. All the hats here are inspired by our time on pristine Block Island, a place that the Nature Conservancy calls one of the "last great places in the western hemisphere."

The clever and colorful hats in this collection are the result of my beloved students—now dear friends—so hardworking and curious, coming together in a peaceful oceanside venue, sharing their love of yarn, knitting, and nature.

Each designer has striven to present her best pattern, each written in her own style, each using a favorite yarn. Feel free to substitute your own favorite fibers and yarns in these projects! This book is a rare treasure. We hope that you will have the pleasure of making many of these patterns for yourself, family, and friends!

Deborah Newton
Spring, 2024

Deborah Newton prepares to release a House Finch at a bird-banding demonstration on Block Island.

Above: Kim Gaffett, licensed bird bander at The Nature Conservancy's Block Island banding station bands a Gray Catbird in the banding room. *Below left:* Kim passes a bird to Deborah to release back to the wild. *Below right:* Kim holds a female Eastern Towhee (formerly called "Rufous-sided Towhee"). *Facing page:* Kim talks to the knitters about the work done at the bird-banding station.

The Nature Conservancy Banding Station

One of the popular activities (besides knitting!) for designers who attend Deborah Newton's Knitwear Design Workshops is visiting the Block Island banding station, run by licensed bird-bander and Nature Conservancy naturalist, Kim Gaffett. Because of where Block Island is located (12 miles from the southern coast of Rhode Island), the Island attracts birds during migration who are looking for a place to rest during their journey. According to Kim, birds—most of whom migrate at night—prefer to travel along the coast so they can drop down to land in the morning to rest and refuel. But sometimes they are pushed off course by strong winds. When that happens, they find themselves over open water and with no place to land. Block Island can serve as an important migration stop for birds who have been blown off-track.

In the morning, Kim sets out soft "mist-nets" to gently catch the birds. Then she weighs each bird and records information about its health (weight, amount of fat) and other data, attaches a lightweight band that has a number marked on it, and then releases the bird to continue on its journey. The data is sent to the national Bird-banding Laboratory at the Patuxent Wildlife Research Center, where scientists around the world are able to access the data to study topics such as bird migration, molting, and population changes.

The Block Island bird-banding facility was first opened in 1967 by Elise Lapham at her home, and she operated it until just a few years before her death in 2011 at age 99.

"Bird-banding is an apprenticeship occupation," said Gaffett. "I banded birds with Elise for 30 years, and during that time she taught me everything I know. Elise was an active community member on Block Island. In addition to banding birds, she was a gardener, educator, dedicated conservationist to birds and the natural world, mother, and grandmother."

Gaffett added that since opening the station in 1967, more than 100,000 birds of 162 species have been banded there, and the station is one of the longest-running stations in North America. "This was only possible due to Lapham's great care of the natural world and protecting the habitats that birds so desperately depend on for survival," she said. "Elise and her husband worked with The Nature Conservancy and the State of Rhode Island to place 140 acres of their land into permanent conservation easement to protect it from future development. Elise the educator, believed that showing people birds in the hand would make them care more about birds and their conservation. Because of this the banding station is available to the public, ready to inspire future birders and wildlife scientists."

The designers of this book are honored to have had the opportunity to watch and participate in bird-banding, and are delighted to be donating all proceeds from the sale of this book to The Nature Conservancy to support the Block Island bird-banding station. Please view the video, "Stopover: Bird-banding on Block Island" to watch and learn from Kim about bird-banding on Block Island.

Abbreviations used in this book

AC	Accent color
beg	Begin/Beginning
BOR	Beginning of round
CC	Contrasting color
CC1	Contrasting color 1 (used when there is more than one contrasting color, e.g., CC2, CC3, etc.)
CDD	Center Double Decrease: Slip two stitches to right needle as if to knit two together. Knit the next stitch. Then, insert left needle as if to purl into the two slipped stitches, and pass them over the knitted stitch.
cm	Centimeter(s)
CO	Cast on
dec	Decrease
dpn(s)	Double-pointed needles(s)
EOR	End of round or end of row
g	Gram(s)
in	Inch(es)
inc	Increase
K	Knit
K1B	Knit one below
K2tog	Knit two stitches together (decreases 1 stitch)
KFB	Knit into front and back of same st (increases 1 stitch)
m	Meter(s)
M1	Make one stitch
MC	Main color
MC1	Main color 1 (used when there is more than one main color, e.g., MC 1, MC2, MC3, etc.)
MB	Make bobble
mm	millimeter(s)
pat	pattern
P	Purl
PM	Place Marker
rep	Repeat
RLDD	Right-leaning, knit-one-below double decrease
rnd	Round
RS	Right side (the side that will face the public)
S1B	Slip one below
Sl	Slip (Sl1 or Sl 1=Slip 1, Sl 2 or Sl2=Slip 2, etc.)
SM	Slip marker
SSK	Slip 2 sts knitwise one at a time to right needle, insert left needle tip into fronts of sts from left to right. Knit the sts together (decrease)
st(s)	Stitch(es)
SS	Stockinette stitch
TBL	Through the back loop
WS	Wrong side (the side that the public will not see)
wyib	With yarn in back
wyif	With yarn in front
yd	Yard(s)

The Hats

Beach Rose Beanie

In Fingering Yarn

Designer: **Deb Frazier**
Ravelry: **Debdidit**
Instagram: **dfrazier2648**

The Beach Rose Beanie is inspired by the vibrant and fragrant mainstay of the dunes and homes of New England beaches, *Rosa rugosa*. From June to August these hearty shrubs decorate the dunes with their bright blossoms, and In the fall, you can harvest the bright red rose hips for jam or teas. You can wear the Beach Rose Beanie in winter to bring back memories of warm sun, and sand between your toes. This design is dedicated to the memory my friend Leigh, lover of the ocean and all things woolly.

SIZE(S)
Small (Medium, Large), to fit head circumference 19 (21, 23) in

HAT MEASUREMENTS
Height, lower edge to tip: 8 in (short hat), 11 in (slouchy hat, above)

MATERIALS

Yarn
1 skein each color Knit Picks Palette Yarn (100% Highland Wool); 231 yd / 50g, in colors as follows:
  MC1: Blue (#23722)
  MC2: Sky (#6882)
  CC1: White (#23728)
  CC2: Pool (#23723)
  CC3: Edamame (#24257)
  CC4: Cotton Candy (#24569)
  CC5: Cosmopolitian(#24568)
  CC6: Canary (# 25531)

Needles
U.S size 2 (2.25 mm, 16-in circular needle
U.S. size 2 dpns, or size to obtain given gauge (NOTE: dpns can be used throughout instead of circular needle if desired).
Yarn needle for weaving in ends.

GAUGE
In Beach Rose and Wave patterns (on page 11) with size 2 needles: 31 sts and 32 rows or rnds = 4 in, knit in the round and blocked.
To save time, take time to check your gauge.

NOTES
1. Hat is worked in the round.
2. This hat can be made into a shorter cap by eliminating several repeats. These instructions are written in green.
3. Skills required: knitting with three colors per rnd, catching floats, corrugated ribbing, making a pompom/tassel.

INSTRUCTIONS

Ribbing
Using size 2, 16-in circular needle, CO 152 (166, 180) sts using Blue (MC1), taking care not twist stitches when joining in the round. Place stitch marker.

Work corrugated K2, P2 rib with Pool (CC2) as the purl stitch for 6 rows. Switch Pool (CC2) to Sky (MC2) for 6 rnds.

This makes 1 in of ribbing. For larger size hats, you may want to make the ribbing a little longer, perhaps 9, or 10 rnds of each color.

Body of hat

Knit 2 rnds of Blue (MC1), increase 2 stitches on either side of the stitch marker on the second row of blue—154 (168, 182) stitches.

Beg at right of chart, knit Wave Chart from page 11, adding stitch markers as needed, every 14 stitches.

Knit Beach Rose Chart #1 from page 11

Knit Wave Chart from page 11

Knit Beach Rose Chart #2 from page 11

Stop here and follow directions for short hat decreases if you want a short cap, continue for slouchy beanie.

Knit Wave Chart.

Knit Beach Rose Chart #1

Knit Wave Chart with these changes:

- Dec 7 stitches evenly on Rnd 3 of Wave chart (it helps to take out stitch markers): 147 (161,175) stitches
- Work the rest of the Wave chart up to Rnd 9
- Dec 7 stitches evenly around Rnd 9: 140 (154, 168) stitches
- Finish Wave chart

Decrease for crown

Next rnd: Using CC2 (Pool), * K12, K2tog; repeat from *

Next rnd: * K11, K2tog; repeat from *

Continue to decrease as described for a total 9 rows

Switch color to Sky (MC2). Continue decreasing as established until you have 7 stitches. Bind off by threading tail through the stitches and tying off inside the hat.

*Short hat crown decreases:

After Beach Rose Chart #2, Knit 2 rnds of CC3 (Edamame)

Knit 5 rnds MC1 (Blue)

Switch to CC2 (Pool)

Next rnd: * K12, k2tog; rep from *

Continue decreases for 5 rnds

Switch to MC2 (Sky) and continue decreasing until you have 7 stitches

Bind off by threading yarn tail through the stitches and tying off inside the hat

FINISHING

Weave in yarn ends. Steam block on a bowl or styrofoam head.

Make a pompom or tassel if desired and attach to top of hat.

Above: Beach Rose Beanie, short version in a monochromatic palette.

ABOUT THE DESIGNER: *Deb Frazier*

I live in Framingham, Massachusetts, with my husband, Lawson, who is an accomplished wild-life photographer. We are surrounded by six cats, one dog, chickens and honeybees, as well as a large garden. My background is in children's illustration and I love a fun and quirky design! I draw inspiration from my surroundings: the changing colors of the garden and organic shapes, the forest and birds that frequent the yard. I love working with color and combinations, often testing them out with a quick watercolor painting or sketch. Top-down colorwork yoke designs are my current obsession.

STITCH PATTERNS

Wave Chart

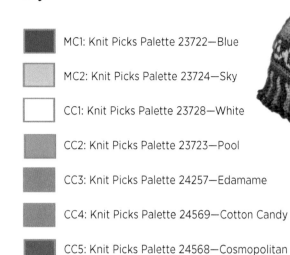

Key

■	MC1: Knit Picks Palette 23722—Blue
■	MC2: Knit Picks Palette 23724—Sky
□	CC1: Knit Picks Palette 23728—White
■	CC2: Knit Picks Palette 23723—Pool
■	CC3: Knit Picks Palette 24257—Edamame
■	CC4: Knit Picks Palette 24569—Cotton Candy
■	CC5: Knit Picks Palette 24568—Cosmopolitan
■	CC6: Knit Picks Palette 255431—Canary

Above: Beach Rose Beanie, short version.

Beach Rose Chart #1

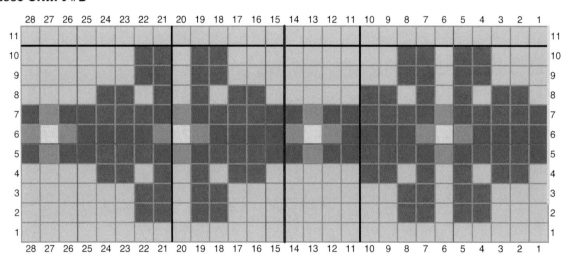

Beach Rose Chart #2

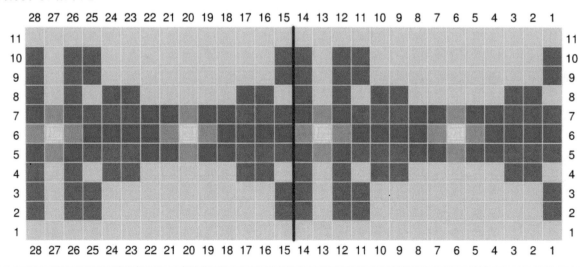

© Diane Tessaglia-Hymes

Winter Wave

In Worsted Yarn **4** MEDIUM

Designer: **Lauren B. Altieri**
Ravelry: **Voila**
Instagram: **@knitterweavermaker**

This is a soft, warm hat for those cold winter days. The colors and design remind me of the ocean waves of Maine.

SIZE

One size fits average adult head.

HAT MEASUREMENTS

Circumference at lower edge: approx. 16 in (unstretched)

Height: 8 in

MATERIALS

Yarn

1 skein each Malibrigo Rios yarn (or worsted weight yarn to meet gauge); 100% superwash merino wool; 210 yd (192 m) / 100 g in colors as follows:

   MC: Cian (#683)
   CC1: Ankara Green (#413)
   CC2: Cucumber (#708)

Needles

Two 16-in circular needles, U.S. sizes 4 and 6
Tapestry needle to weave in ends.

GAUGE

In ribbing with size 4 needles: 26 sts and 4 rnds = 4 in
In pattern with size 6 needles: 25 sts and 4 rnds = 4 in
To save time, take time to check your gauge.

NOTES

1. Hat is worked in the round, brim to crown, starting with ribbing.
2. **Hint**: To decrease the number of ends to weave in at the end, the colors can be alternately carried up the beginning of each rnd.

INSTRUCTIONS

Ribbing

With MC and size 4 needles, CO 104 stitches using long-tail cast-on method. Join to knit in the rnd, making sure not to twist stitches.

Work in rnds of K1, P1 rib for 1½ inches

Change to size 6 needles and K 1 row.

Main section of hat

Starting with CC1, knit 4 rnds of Winter Wave pattern on page 14

Continue in pattern, work 4 rnds with CC2, and then work 4 rnds with MC.

Repeat the pattern and color changes until hat measures 6 in from beginning.

Crown Shaping

With MC, begin crown shaping as follows:

Rnd 1: *K6, K2tog; rep from * (91 sts)
Rnd 2: K
Rnd 3: *K5, K2tog; rep from * (78 sts)
Rnd 4: K
Rnd 5: *K4, K2tog; rep from * (65 sts)
Rnd 6: K
Rnd 7: *Knit 3, K2tog; rep from * (52 sts)
Rnd 6: K
Rnd 7: *K2, K2tog; rep from * (39 sts)
Rnd 8: K
Rnd 9: *K1, K2tog (26 sts)

Rnd 10: K

Rnd 11: K2tog around (13 sts)

FINISHING

Cut the yarn, leaving an 8-in tail. Thread the needle with the tail of yarn. Draw the needle through 13 live stitches, then close. Fasten off and weave in all ends. Wet block to finish. Add a pompom if desired.

STITCH PATTERN

Winter Wave Pattern stitch

Multiple of 4 sts

Rnd 1: *K1 sl 3; repeat from *

Rnd 2: K2, sl 1 *K3, sl 1; repeat from * to last stitch, K1

Rnd 3: K

Rnd 4: K

Rep Rnds 1–4

Note: this pattern is adapted from: "Tricolor Wave Stripes" pattern in Barbara Walker's *Treasury of Knitting Patterns*. School House Press, 1988. p55.

©Deborah Newton

A view of the North Lighthouse in the distance.

ABOUT THE DESIGNER: *Lauren B. Altieri*

Lauren is a fiber enthusiast who loves the magic of knitting. She always has something on her needles and loves learning new tips, tricks and techniques. New England is her home where she enjoys the many sheep and wool events to explore new fibers. The fiber content or color will inspire her to try a new stitch pattern or color combinations. You can find her on Ravelry as Voila.

Cassio Hat

In Fingering Yarn 2 FINE

Designer: **Teema Loeffelholz**
Ravelry: **TeemasTextiles**

This circular hat is inspired by the elk herd that lives in Bridger Canyon, Montana. The design combines traditional Fair Isle motifs with antlers in a creative and colorful combination. This hat was knitted in Jumper Weight Yarn from Jamieson and Smith, a Shetland Wool from the Shetland Islands. Using a wooly yarn is helpful to accomplish the shape and weight that makes this hat fit perfectly.

SIZE

One size fits all.

HAT MEASUREMENT

Approx. 20-in circumference x 6.75-in height before blocking.

MATERIALS

Yarn

1 skein each of 2-ply Jumper Weight yarn from Jamieson and Smith (100% wool); 115m (125yds) / 25g in colors as follows (numbers indicate the colors used in the sample)

Background colors
MC1: 202 (light)
MC2: 3 (medium)
MC3: FC64 (dark)

Accent color
AC: 82

Pattern colors
CC1: 72 (light)

CC2: 9113 (medium)
CC3: FC 13 (dark)

Needles

U.S size 1.5 (2.5 mm) 16-in long circular needle
Four U.S size 1.5 (2.5 mm) dpns, or size to obtain given gauge.
Yarn needle for weaving in ends

GAUGE

32 sts and 32 rows to 4 in (10 cm) in SS
To save time, take time to check your gauge.

NOTES

1. This hat will fit snugly on a 23-in head; adjust the needle size down for a smaller fit or up for a larger fit to accommodate the desired size.
2. If desired, dpns can be used throughout instead of a circular needle.

INSTRUCTIONS

Ribbing

With needle to obtain the correct gauge and using AC, cast on 100 sts, place marker, and join for working in the round, taking care not to twist stitches when joining.

Following Cassio Ribbing Chart on page 19, work 14 rnds of P2–K2 ribbing.

Main section of hat

Row 15: Using MC3, knit row, increasing 60 sts evenly as follows: K1, (M1, K1) 10 times, (M1, K2) 39 times, (M1, K1) 10 times, M1, k1.

Row 16: Begin Cassio Main Chart on page 19, taking

extra care with establishing correct pattern in the first few rnds; there are four pattern repeats consisting of 40 sts each.

Body of hat

Starting with Rnd 1 with colors MC3 and AC, work each rnd of chart reading right to left and repeating pattern 4 times total.

Continue to follow pattern, changing colors as shown on Cassio Main Chart.

Crown of hat

The crown is designed for dark colors to be knit on top of light colors and vice versa.

To maintain alternating colors for the crown, start each row with colors indicated by the Cassio Crown Chart on page 19 and proceed by maintaining the alternating color pattern based on the color below.

This will change after decreases, requiring some rows to decrease in one color and then repeat that same color once because the stitch below requires it.

After the first repeat and decrease, use the color of the stitch below to determine which color puts a light on top of a dark or a dark on top of a light to maintain the alternating pattern for the crown of the hat.

Rnd 56: * K16, PM; repeat from * to last 16 sts. Be sure to distinguish section markers from BOR marker.

Rnd 57: * K15, K2tog, slip marker; rep from *

Rnd 58: * K14, K2tog, slip marker; rep from *

Rnd 59: * K13, K2tog, slip marker; rep from *

Rnd 60: * K12, K2tog, slip marker; rep from *

Rnd 61: * K11, K2tog, slip marker; rep from *

Rnd 62: * K10, K2tog, slip marker; rep from *

Rnd 63: * K9, K2tog, slip marker; rep from *

Rnd 64: * K8, K2tog, slip marker; rep from *

Rnd 65: * K7, K2tog, slip marker; rep from *

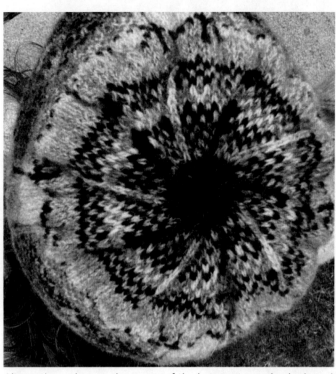

Alternating colors on the crown of the hat creates a checkerboard pattern.

Rnd 66: * K6, K2tog, slip marker; rep from *

Rnd 67: * K5, K2tog, slip marker; rep from *

Rnd 68: * K4, K2tog, slip marker; rep from *

Rnd 69: * K3, K2tog, slip marker; rep from *

Rnd 70: * K2, K2tog, slip marker; rep from *

Rnd 71: * K1, K2tog, slip marker ; rep from *

Rnd 72: * K2tog, slip marker; rep from * Break yarn with enough to secure the remaining stitches with the yarn needle.

FINISHING

Weave in ends.

Wet block: gently submerge the hat in warm water and wool wash for several minutes; remove from the bath without stretching any part of the hat and press flat between towels to remove water. Lay flat to dry.

ABOUT THE DESIGNER: *Teema Loeffelholz*

Teema resides in the picturesque Bridger Canyon, Montana, where she immerses herself in the mountain lifestyle that inspires her daily. An aspiring talent in the realm of textiles, Teema is dedicated to the art of knitwear design, weaving, and textile creation. Her passion is not just a personal journey; it's a communal venture. She is at the helm of launching Gallatin Valley Fiber House, a venture aimed at enriching her community by offering an array of fiber-related educational events. Teema believes in the transformative power of fiber arts and is committed to sharing this with her community, ensuring that the warmth and creativity of fiber arts can be experienced by all who wish to explore it.

STITCH PATTERN

Cassio Ribbing Chart

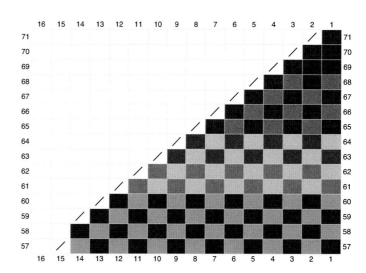

Key

	K with MC1: 202 (light)
	K with MC2: 3 (medium)
	K with MC3: FC64 (dark)
	K with AC: 82
○	P with AC: 82
	K with CC1: 72 (light)
	K with CC2: 9113 (medium)
	K with CC3: FC 13 (dark)
╱	K2tog

Cassio Crown Chart

Cassio Main Chart

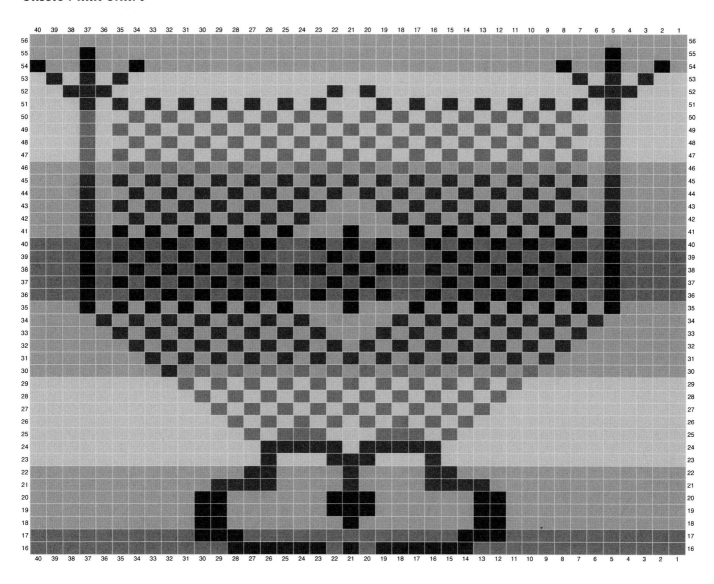

Waves at Grace's Cove Hat

In Worsted Yarn **4 MEDIUM**

Designer: **Barbara Hyland-Hill**
Ravelry: **knitwit3**

This hat is worked in an easy-to-memorize textured pattern that creates visual waves. The waves are reminiscent of the waves seen during sunsets on the beautiful beach at Grace's Cove on Block Island.

SIZE(S)

Small, (Medium, Large), to fit head circumference of 18–20 (20–22, 22–24) in

HAT MEASUREMENTS

Circumference around body of hat (4 in from edge): approximately 17 (19, 21) in unstretched and laid flat.

Height, lower edge to tip: 7-½ (8-½, 9-½) inches laid flat

MATERIALS

Yarn

1 skein for each size of Cadence from Hazel Knits; 100% Superwash Merino; 220 yd (200 m) / 110 g.

Colors and quantities used:
   Small: Satin Slip (pink) 70 g
   Medium: Cornflower (blue) 90 g
   Large: Graphite (gray) 110 g

Needles

Sizes U.S. size 5 (3.75 mm) and U.S. 7 (4.50 mm) 16-in circular needles or 32-in cable for magic loop, or needle size to obtain given gauge (note: dpns may be used throughout instead of circular needle if desired).

Notions

Stitch markers (at least two colors)
Yarn needle for weaving in ends

GAUGE

In Wave Textured Pattern (see page 22), with larger size needles: 22 sts and 32 rnds = 4 in
To save time, take time to check your gauge.

NOTES

1. Hat is worked in the round from brim to crown.
2. Use a stitch marker in one color to note beginning of the round.
3. Place stitch markers in a different color every 11 stitches to separate each repeat of the wave pattern for ease in following the pattern repeats.
4. Suggest using the Twisted German Cast On which is quick and provides a nice elastic edge. (See Twisted German Cast On by Andrea Mowry)

INSTRUCTIONS

CO 98 (110, 120) sts on the U.S. 5 (3.75 mm) circular needles using the Twisted German Cast On.
Join work in the round, being careful that the cast-on edge is not twisted. Place marker for the beginning of the round.

Ribbing

Work in K1, P1 ribbing for 1-½ in.

For sizes Small and Large: On the last rnd of ribbing, work to 2 sts before marker, KFB in K st, P last st (1 st increased. Small=99 sts, Large=121 sts)

Main section of hat

Set-up Rounds

Change to U.S. size 7 (4.50 mm) circular needles

Small   Medium   Large

Rnd 1: Purl.

Rnd 2: * K 11 place marker; repeat from * 7 (8, 9) more times, then K 11 before BOR marker for a total of 9 (10, 11) pattern sections.

(Section markers should be a different color from the BOR marker).

Wave Textured Pattern

Rnds 1, 3: P

Rnds 2, 5, 7, 9: K

Rnds 4, 6, 8, 10: * K2tog, K2, KFB next 2 sts, K3, SSK; repeat from * to end of rnd

Repeat pattern Rnds 1–10 for a total of 3 (4, 5) times.

Work Rnds 1–3 once more for all sizes.

Hat should measure approximately 6 (7.25 , 8.5) in from brim edge

Crown of hat

Work crown shaping as follows:

Rnd 1: * K2tog work to 2 sts before section marker, SSK* repeat for each section. 81 (90, 99) sts

Rnds 2, 4, 6, 9, 12: K

Rnd 3: * K3, sl 2 sts together knitwise to righthand needle, K next st, pass both sl sts over K st, K3; repeat from * for each section. 63 (70, 77) sts

Rnd 5: * K2tog, K3, SSK; repeat from * for each section. 45 (50, 55) sts

Rnd 7: * K1, sl 2sts together knitwise to righthand needle, K next st, pass both sl sts over K st, K1; repeat from * for each section. 27 (30, 33) sts

Rnds 8, 10: Purl

Rnd 11: * K1, K2tog; repeat from * in each section—18 (20, 22) sts

Rnd 13: K2tog around. 9 (10, 11) sts

Rnd 14: K2tog around; Sizes small and large will have 1 st left over after decreases; knit last st. 5 (5, 6) sts

Break the yarn and pull through the remaining sts on the needle.

FINISHING

Weave in all ends.

Lightly steam the body of the hat, but avoid steaming the ribbing.

A pompom can be attached if desired.

ABOUT THE DESIGNER: *Barbara Hyland-Hill*

Barbara is a retired nurse executive living in Seattle with her husband. Knitting has been a lifelong passion since learning to knit as a child. Barbara's love of fiber, texture, color—and the fabric these elements can create—challenges her exploration of new techniques and various knitting genres. She enjoys knitting garments and accessories while benefiting from the meditative quality of knitting. She looks forward to what has become the annual trek to Block Island. Participating in Deborah Newton's design workshops and interacting with other fiber enthusiasts has been truly inspirational.

The view of the Atlantic Ocean from the second floor of the 1661 Inn.

Manisses Hues Hat

In DK Yarn **3 LIGHT**

Designer: **Brenda Hyland-Miller**
Ravelry: **hylandmiller**

Manisses Hues translates to "Block Island colors." Manisses is the Narragansett Indian name for Block Island. This lined hat is warm against the sea breeze and has a simple "Blocks of Island" colored pattern. The hat is worked in the round. This pattern works well with two contrasting colors, a solid and variegated yarn, two solid colors, using mini skeins, or leftover stash yarns. I picked colors inspired by the island's hues.

SIZE(S)

(Infant, Child, Youth) [Women, Men, Extra-large] to fit head circumference (14, 16, 18) [20, 22, 24] inches.

HAT MEASUREMENTS

Circumference at lower edge: (14,16,18) [20,22,24] in
Height, lower edge to tip: (7, 8, 9)[10, 11, 12] in

MATERIALS

Yarn

1 skein each yarn color, as follows:

Hat 1 (above)

MC: Schwolle Zauberball Edition 3, Color 3 2298_ Laundry Day, 150m (164 yds) / 50 g, 100% virgin wool (fine merino), washable
CC: Schwolle Zauberball Edition 3, color 2511_All inclusive, 150 m, (164 yds) / 50g, 100% Virgin wool (fine merino) washable

Hat 2 (left)

MC: Hazel Knits hand-dyed, Nekkid Artisan Sock, 90% superwash merino, 10% nylon 440 yards/120 g.

CC: Hazel Knits hand-dyed, "Pride Rainbow" Artisan Sock Color Play Set (six 133-yd skeins 90% superwash merino, 10% nylon) plus one mini skein of Glacier Artisan Sock (133 yards).

Needles

U.S. sizes 4 and 5, 16-in circular needles, or four size 4 and 5 dpns, or size to obtain given gauge (note: dpns can be used throughout instead of circular needle if desired)

Notions

Yarn needle for weaving in ends

GAUGE

For lining: Using size 4 needles, 27 sts and 36 rows or rounds = 4 inches in stockinette stitch

For colorwork: Using size 5 needles 24 sts and 33 rows or rounds = 4 inches in pattern.

To save time, take time to check your gauge.

INSTRUCTIONS

Hat lining

With smaller needles and MC, cast on (85, 100, 115) [130, 145, 160] st using long tail cast-on, join in the round, avoid twisting stitches. Place BOR marker.

The lined hat circumference should match your head circumference. (14, 16, 18) [20, 22, 24] in. If your head size is between hat sizes, go up a size.

Knit the lining in stockinette stitch for (2.5, 2.75, 3.25} [3.5, 3.75, 4] in

Main section of hat

Change to larger needles. Knit a purl row, knit 2 rows in SS.

With MC and CC work the Manisses Hues chart at right until the lining is the same length as the body. Fold along the purl row edge, matching the lining and body lengths.

Join lining and body

While continuing to work the Manisses Hues chart pattern, knit into the stitch on the left needle and pick up an edge stitch on the lining, knit both stitches together, repeat until BOR marker.

Repeat the chart (4, 5, 6) [7, 8, 9] times or until hat measures (6.5, 7.5, 8.50) (9, 9.5, 10) in. from lower edge, or until desired length.

Crown of hat

Rnd 1: CDD, K1 around: (43,50,57) [66,73,80] sts remaining

Rnd 2: K

Rnd 3: CDD around: (21,24,29) [33,37,40] sts remaining

Rnd 4: K2tog around: (6,6,7) [8,9,10] sts remaining

FINISHING

Cut yarn leaving a 6-in. tail. Using a tapestry needle, thread the tail through the remaining sts, closing the opening. Weave in ends on wrong side of hat. Steam block or use alternative blocking approach based on yarn used. A pompom can be added to the top of the hat, if desired.

Brenda releases an Eastern Towhee at the Nature Conservancy's bird-banding station on Block Island.

STITCH PATTERN

Manisses Hues Chart

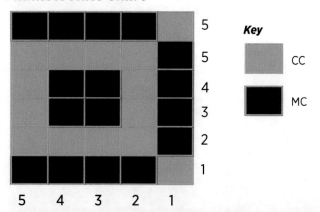

Key

CC

MC

Yarn used for above hats—1 skein each yarn color, as follows: *Hat 1:* see p. 22 (snap-on faux-fur pink pompom by Ivy Brambles, Knitting with Friends). *Hat 2:* see p. 22. *Hat 3:* (MC) Hazel Knits, hand-dyed, Artisan Sock, color Moonshadow; (CC) Hazel Knits hand-dyed Artisan sock mini skeins, colors Jellyfish, Electric Liliac, Icecle, Thistle, Nekkid. *Hat 4:* (MC) The Fibre Co., Amble, color Blackbeck; (CC) Schwolle Zauberball Edition 3, Color 3 2521.

ABOUT THE DESIGNER: Brenda Hyland-Miller

I love to knit sweaters and gifts that let me experiment with color, texture, techniques, styles, fiber, and construction. For the past few years, I have been learning to design from Deborah Newton. She has expanded my creative mindset and knitting experience. My goal is simple: to learn something new with each project, enjoy the creative process, and knit beautiful, well-fitting garments. Spending time with knitting friends is a valued bonus.

The Manisses Inn on Block Island.

28

Round the Island Hat

In DK Yarn  **3** LIGHT

Designer: **Jennifer Curly Girl**
Ravelry: **jenniferwalsh**
Website: **jennifercurlygirl.com**

On the trail or under sail, the Round the Island Hat keeps you warm for all your adventures! The simple two-color circle pattern with fun bobbles on the ribbing can be made using many different color combinations of DK-weight yarn.

SIZES
Baby/Newborn (Child S/Toddler, Child L/Adult S) (Adult M, Adult L)

HAT MEASUREMENTS
Circumference: 13¼ (16, 18¼) (20½, 22¾) in [33.5 (40.5, 46.25) (52, 57.75) cm]
Height: 7 (8, 9½) (10¼, 10¾) in [15.25 (20.25, 24) (26, 27.25) cm]
Note: Refer to a hat that fits you well to choose your size.

MATERIALS

Yarn
DK weight yarn, two colors, approximately 200–250 yards (183–230 m) each

Size Baby/Newborn (above right)
KOIGI Kersti Merino Crepe (100% Merino Wool), hand painted Dye Lots
Color A: K2174 11 (dark blue)
Color B: K2171.5 3 (light blue)

Size Child S/ Toddler (page 31)
Color A: Tina's Toasty Toes Toasty DK (100% Superwash Merino Wool) Warm Hearts (Pink)
Color B: Schowhouse Yarns (100% Superwash Merino Wool) OOAK Orange Specks (Yellow)

Size Child L/Adult S (page 28)
Color A: Knits EIEI Wools (100% Superwash Merino, 4 ply DK), Plymouth Harbor Blues (dark)
Color B: The Fiber Seed Sprout DK (90% Washable American Merino Wool, 10% Nylon) Arctic (light)

Size Adult M (above left)
Madeline Tosh, Tosh DK, 100% Superwash Merino Wool
Color A: Iris (purple)
Color B: Sugar Coat (white)

Needles
U.S. size 5 (3.75 mm) circular needle
U.S. size 5 (3.75 mm) dpns
darning needle

GAUGE
21 sts and 25 rows = 4 in, using U.S. size 5 needles in stockinette stitch

NOTES
1. When a strand of yarn (float) will extend over more than 6 stitches, trap it with the working yarn. Here is a helpful explanation for trapping floats.
2. Floats should be carried loosely across the WS.
3. The decreases for the crown of the hat happen in the first round of each new Circle Pattern.
4. The Transition Rounds are done at the same time as you are knitting the color pattern.

INSTRUCTIONS

Lower Edge Ribbing with Bobbles [6 rows]
Using Color A and the long tail cast on, CO 72 (84,

96) (108, 120) sts

Rnd 1: Join in the round. *K3, P3; rep from * to EOR

Repeat Rnd 1 two more times.

Bobble Rnd: *K3, P1, MB, P1; rep from * to EOR. (See below for instructions, or watch this video about how to make a bobble.)

Repeat Rnd 1 two more times.

Main Section of Hat

Join Color B

Work 7-Row Circle Pattern (7 rows): 3 (4, 5) (5, 5) times

At this point the hat measures 4½ (5½, 6¾) (6¾, 6¾) in [11.5 (14, 17) (17, 17) cm] and the **Transition Rnd** decreases begin with each new circle pattern.

Work these **Transition Rnds** on the *first rnd only* of a new circle pattern:

- **6-Row Circle Pattern:** *K2, K2tog, K2; rep from * to EOR
- **4-Row Circle Pattern:** *K2tog, K3; rep from * to EOR
- **3-Row Circle Pattern:** *K2tog, K2; rep from * to EOR

Work 6-Row Circle Pattern (6 rows): 1 (1, 1) (1, 1) times

Work 4-Row Circle Pattern (4 rows): 1 (1, 1) (2, 2) times

Work 3-Row Circle Pattern (3 rows): 1 (1, 1) (1, 2) times [36 (42, 48) (54, 60)] sts

Crown

The crown of the hat uses only Color A.

Size Baby/Newborn only

Rnd 1: K

Rnd 2: *K2tog, K1; rep from * to EOR

Rnd 3: *K2tog, K1; rep from * to EOR

Rnd 4: *K2tog; rep from * to EOR

Size Child S/Toddler only

Rnd 1: K

Rnd 2: *K2tog, K1; rep from * to EOR

Rnd 3: *K2tog; rep from * to EOR

Rnd 4: K2, *K2tog; rep from * to EOR

Size Child L/Adult S size only

Rnd 1: K

Rnd 2 *K2tog, K1; rep from * to EOR

Rnd 3: K

Rnd 4: *K2tog; rep from * to EOR

Rnd 5: K

Rnd 6: *K2tog; rep from * to EOR

Size Adult M only

Rnd 1: K

Rnd 2: *K2tog, K1; rep from * to EOR

Rnd 3: K

Rnd 4: *K2tog, K1; rep from * to EOR

Rnd 5: *K2tog, K1; rep from * to EOR

Rnd 6: *K2tog; rep from * to EOR

Size Adult L only

Rnd 1: K

Rnd 2: *K2tog, K1; rep from * to EOR

Rnd 3: K

Rnd 4: *K2tog, K3; rep from * to EOR

Rnd 5: *K2tog; rep from * to EOR

Rnd 6: *K2tog; rep from * to EOR

All sizes

Break yarn, leaving an 8-in tail. Using a darning needle, thread yarn through the remaining 8 sts twice and pull tight.

FINISHING

Block hat and weave in all ends.

Make a pompom using equal amounts of both colors

ABOUT THE DESIGNER: *Jennifer Curly Girl*

I am based in the Boston area, where I am never far from the beautiful coast or the majestic mountains. For fun, I spend time sailing, hiking, skiing, doing yoga, and picking flowers. These activities provide me with inspiration for my designs. Not only am I finding ideas in the natural world, I am also contemplating and meditating on how these ideas become actual designs. Mostly, I am working on sweaters but there is always a hat, sock, or shawl pattern ready to get on my·needles.

and attach to the top of the hat. Here is a <u>helpful video about making a pompom with your hands</u>. The pompom for all sizes is wrapped 100 times around two fingers.

TECHNIQUES AND STITCH PATTERNS

Make Bobble [MB]

1. K1, YO, K1, YO, K1 (all in one st). There are now 5 bobble sts to work over the next 4 rows. Turn work.

2. P1, P1 TBL, P1, P1 TBL, P1, turn work

3. K5, turn work

4. P5, turn work

5. K5, *using tip of left needle, slip second st over first on right needle; rep from * three times (bobble is now one single stitch).

Circle Stitch Patterns

Each box in the charts below represents one stitch and each row in the charts represents one round. The charts should be read from right to left and repeated across the round. When starting a new round, start again at the right side of the chart and work to the left. The red line in the chart outlines the single repeat for each pattern. The charts are shown here with two repeats of the pattern to show the color changes.

7-Row Circle Pattern

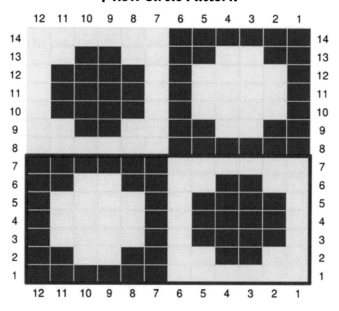

6-Row Circle Pattern

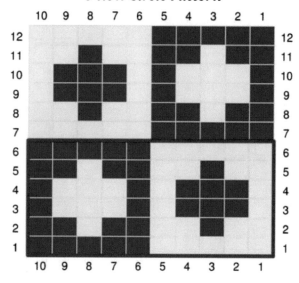

4-Row Circle Pattern

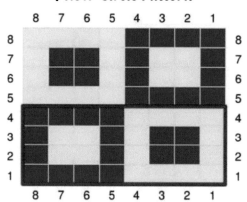

3-Row Circle Pattern

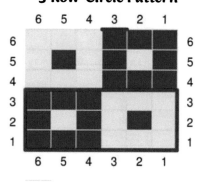

Key

Color B (light blue)

Color A (dark blue)

31

Ruched Beret

In DK Yarn **3 LIGHT**

Designer: **Kitty Savel**
Ravelry: **FibrForwrdDesigns**

The texture of this hat is created by "ruching"—doubling stitches in one row, and then quickly decreasing back to the starting amount a few rows later.

SIZES
One size fits most.

HAT MEASUREMENTS
Band circumference: Fits 18–23 in
Circumference at widest part: 11 in

MATERIALS

Yarn
1 skein Cascade Blue Faced Leicester yarn; 100% Wool, 262 yd (240 m) / 100g (3.5 oz), or another DK/Light Worsted yarn to get the given gauge.

Needles
U.S. size 7 (4.50mm) and size 9 (5.50mm) 24 in (60mm) circular needles or size needed to get gauge.
U.S. size 7 (4.50mm) and size 9 (5.50mm) dpns (sets of five) or size needed to get gauge.

GAUGE
20 stitches and 26 rows = 4 in using smaller size needles or size needed to get gauge.

INSTRUCTIONS
Using Size 7 dpns cast on 98 stitches using Cable Cast On method.
Join in the round being careful not to twist stitches. (Divide stitches over four dpns as follows: 25 stitches on 3 of the needles and remaining 23 stitches on another dpn.

Rnds 1-12: *Ki, P1; repeat from * around.

Change to Size 9 circular needles.

Rnd 13: *K14; place marker; , Repeat from * around.

Rnd 14: Knit; slipping markers.

Rnd 15: *K14, M1, slip marker. Repeat from * around. (105 total stitches).

Rnd 16: Knit; slipping markers.

Rnd 17: *K15, M1 slip marker. Repeat from *around. (112 total stitches).

Rnd 18: Knit; slipping markers.

Rnd 19: *K1, M1, slip markers. Repeat from *around (119 total stitches).

Change to Size 7 circular needles.

Rnd 20: *K1, M1 slip marker. Repeat from * around. (There will be 34 stitches between markers).

Rnd 21: *Knit 34, M1. Repeat from *around, slipping markers. (There are 35 stitches between markDers).

Rnd 22: Knit; slipping markers.

Rnd 23: *K35, M1. Repeat from * around, slipping markers. (There are 36 stitches between markers).

Rnd 24: Knit; slipping markers.

Rnd 25: *K36, M1. Repeat from * around, slipping markers. (There are 37 stitches between markers).

Rnd 26: Knit; slipping markers.

Change to Size 9 circular needles.

Rnd 27: K2tog around slipping markers. (There are 19 stitches between markers).

Rnd 28: *K19, M1. Repeat from * around, slipping markers. (There are 20 stitches between markers).

Rnd 29: Knit; slipping markers.

Rnd 30: (Beginning decrease rows) *K18, K2tog. Repeat from *around slipping markers. (There are 19 stitches between markers).

Rnd 31: Knit; slipping markers.

Rnd 32: *K17, K2tog. Repeat from * around slipping markers. (There are 18 stitches between markers.

Rnd 33: Knit; slipping markers.

Change to Size 7 circular needles.

Rnd 34:K1, M1 slip marker. Repeat from * around. (There are 36 stitches between markers).

Rnd 35: *K34, K2tog. Repeat from * around. (There are 35 stitches between markers).

Rnd 36: Knit; slipping markers.

Rnd 37: *K33, K2tog. Repeat from * around. (There are 34 stitches between markers).

Rnd 38: Knit; slipping markers.

Rnd 39: *K32, K2tog. Repeat from * around. (There are 33 stitches between markers).

Rnd 40: Knit; slipping markers.

Change to Size 9 circular needles.

Rnd 41: K2tog around slipping markers. (There are 17 stitches between markers). Continue in following pattern switching to Size 9 double pointed needles when it is difficult to when it becomes difficult to knit with circular needles.

Rnd 42: *K15, K2tog. Repeat from * around. (There are 16 stitches between markers).

Rnd 43: Knit; slipping markers.

Rnd 44: *K14, K2tog. Repeat from * around. (There are 15 stitches between markers).

Rnd 45: Knit; slipping markers.

Rnd 46: *Knit 13, K2tog. Repeat from * around. (There are 14 stitches between markers).

Rnd 47: Knit; slipping markers.

Rnd 48: *Knit 12, K2tog. Repeat from * around. (There are 13 stitches between markers).

Rnd 49: Knit; slipping markers.

Rnd 50: *Knit 11, K2tog. Repeat from * around. (There are 12 stitches between markers).

Rnd 51: Knit; slipping markers.

Rnd 52: *Knit 10, K2tog. Repeat from * around. (There are 11 stitches between markers).

Rnd 53: Knit; slipping markers.

Rnd 54: *Knit 9, K2tog. Repeat from * around. (There are 10 stitches between markers).

Rnd 55: Knit; slipping markers.

Rnd 56: *Knit 8, K2tog. Repeat from * around. (There are 9 stitches between markers).

Rnd 57: Knit; slipping markers.

Rnd 58: Knit 7; K2tog. Repeat from * around. (There are 8 stitches between markers).

Knit the last two rounds until 14 stitches in total remain.

Next Rnd: K2tog around removing markers.

FINISHING
Weave the tail through last 7 stitches on the remaining double pointed needles and fasten off securely. Weave in ends.

ABOUT THE DESIGNER: Kitty Savel

I live in Pennsylvania where I love to knit, crochet and slow stitch. I have started designing my own sweaters and my favorite yarns are merino and mohair. Right now I am working in bulky knits, but I also have plans for designing with worsted weight yarn. This beret hat design which utilizes DK weight yarn came out of my interest in ruching in knitted fabric. It is a technique that is versatile enabling me to use stockinette stitch and incorporate various other knitting stitches with it. I also love other crafts including fabric collage and slow stitching. I have exhibited my work at various museums and art venues across Pennsylvania.

Stones on a Block Island beach.

Block Island Slouchy Striped Hat

In Worsted Yarn **4 MEDIUM**

Designer: **Maureen Cullen**
Ravelry: **cullenmmm**

This slouchy hat is quick and easy! Knit mostly in stockinette, the decreases in the crown make it stand out. It can be finished with pompoms and tassels but looks great as it is. Choose colors that go well together and are favorites, match your outfit, or are even your school colors! This hat looks best with three colors. The fabric and width of the early stripes make this hat a good canvas for adding your own designs through duplicate stitch or embroidery. Put that school name or your favorite sports team's name on the school or team colors!

SIZES

Small (Medium, Large)

MEASUREMENTS

Circumference measured in stockinette stripe is approximately 16 (20, 22) inches. When stretched slightly the ribbed section is approximately the same width.

Note: it is easy to adjust the height of the hat by adjusting the height of the stripes.

MATERIALS

Yarn

Three colors (Color A, Color B, Color C) of Cascade 220 Superwash; 220 yd (200 m) / 100 g (3.5 oz)

Approximately 60 yd of each color is needed for each hat.

Needles

16-in U.S. size 6 circular needle or size needed to obtain gauge.

U.S. size 6 dpns or size needed to obtain gauge.

Notions

1 stitch marker

GAUGE

24 sts and 32 rnds = 4 in. Note: while gauge is not as important in a hat as in a garment, if your gauge is different from what is stated, the size of your hat will be different.

INSTRUCTIONS

For a jogless join, see this video of Patty Lyons' Jogless Join.

Body of hat

Cast on 100 (124, 132) stitches. Join in the round, being careful not to twist stitches.

With color A, work 2 x 2 twisted rib (see page 38 for instructions) for 1¾ (2, 2) in

Change to Color B and knit each rnd for 1-¾ (2, 2) in

Change to Color C and knit each rnd for 1-¾, (2, 2) in

Change to Color A and knit each rnd for 1 in

Change to Color B and knit each rnd for 1 in

Change to Color C and knit each rnde for 1 in

Change to Color A and knit each rnd for ½ in

Change to Color B and knit each rnd for ½ in

Change toColor C and knit each rnd for ½ in

For large size only, dec 2 st evenly in final row of Color C (100 [124, 13] sts)

Crown

Note: in this section it is useful to carry the colors up when changing colors rather than starting a new yarn with each change in color.

Change to color A

Row 1: * (K3, K2tog); rep from * to last 0 (4, 0) stitches, then K2, K2tog (80 [99, 104] sts)

Row 2: Knit

Row 3: * (K3, K2tog); rep from * to last 0 (4, 4) stitches, then K2, K2tog; (64 [79, 83] sts)

Change to color B

Row 4: Knit.

Row 5: * (K3, K2tog); rep from * to the last 4 (4, 3) stitches; then,

    for small size, K2, K2tog (51 sts)

    for medium size, K2tog 2 times (62 sts)

    for large size K1, K2tog-(66 sts)

Row 6: Knit.

Change to color C

Row 7: * (K2, K2tog); rep from * to last 3 (2, 2) sts; then,

    for small size K1, K2tog (38 sts)

    for medium and large sizes K2tog (46, 49 sts)

Row 8: Knit.

Row 9: *(K2, K2tog); rep from * to last 2 (2, 1) sts; then,

    for small and medium sizes, K2tog (28, 34 sts)

    for large size K1 (37 sts)

Change to color A

Row 10: Knit

Change to color B

Row 11: * (K1, K2tog); rep from * to last 1 stitch, end K1 [19 (23, 25) sts]

Change to color C

Row 12: K2tog to last 1 stitch, end K1 [10 (12, 13) sts]

Change to color A

Row 13: K2tog to last 0 (0, 1) st, end K1 [5 (6, 7) sts]

Bring yarn through remaining stitches, gathering them together and tie off.

Weave in all ends, lightly block or steam. Note: to shorten or lengthen the hat, you can change the width of the stripes or increase the number of stripes. Start decreasing only after you have achieved your desired length.

FINISHING

Weave in ends. Add a pompom if desired.

TECHNIQUE

2 x 2 Twisted Rib Stitch

Multiple of 4 sts. On every rnd, * K2 through the back loops, P2; repeat from * to end of rnd.

ABOUT THE DESIGNER: *Maureen Cullen*

Maureen taught herself to knit at 12 years old. While in the workforce, knitting was her way to relax during her careers as CPA and nurse practitioner. Now retired, Maureen finally has time to devote to her love of all things fiber. Three days a week she indulges her passion at her local yarn shop—knitting, helping answer customers' knitting questions, and solving the world's problems with knitting buddies! Design was a natural progression from her desire to learn more. She likes to design projects that beginning and intermediate fiberholics will enjoy and can use as a springboard in their own knitting journey. Maureen lives in New Hampshire with her two labs, where she enjoys traveling and visiting her children and grandchildren.

North Lighthouse, Block Island

The Nessie

In Sport/DK Yarn

3 LIGHT

Designer: **Lynn Murphy**
Ravelry: **tuuvy**
email: **tuuvy50@yahoo.com**

This fun, brimmed summer beach hat is quickly and easily done in simple single crochet, starting at the top. Dress it up by using contrasting textured, sparkling, and/or shiny multicolored yarn for the ribbon band and rose. Version 1 (left) has a shorter brim, and Version 2 (above) has a longer brim.

SIZE

Medium to Large, 22 to 23-in head circumference

MATERIALS:

Yarn

Version 1 (yellow hat, left)

MC: 2 skeins Rowan's Cotton Glace yarn in Ochre #833

CC: 1 skein Tahki's Tandem yarn in Sunburst #028

Version 2 (gray hat, above)

MC: 2 skeins Rowan's Cotton Glace in Dawn Gray #831

CC: 1 skein Sesia's Bluebell yarn in Silver #8436, divided into two equal smaller skeins

Hook and notions

Crochet hook size 2.5 mm

Removable stitch marker

Yarn needle for weaving in ends and for making rose

GAUGE

Using 2.5 mm crochet hook, 6 sc should equal 1 in. (2.5 cm)

NOTES

1. Hat is worked in the round, starting at the crown and working towards the brim.

2. Do not join rounds—just use removable marker to mark last stitch of each round.

CROCHET ABBREVIATIONS

ch	chain
crab st	single crochet in each single crochet going backwards instead of forward
inc	increase. To increase 1 st, work 2 single crochets in same stitch
sc	single crochet

INSTRUCTIONS

Crown (same for Version 1 and 2)

Using MC, ch 3 then join to form a circle with a slip st in first ch.

Rnd 1: 8 sc in the circle, place a removable marker in the last st of every round.

Rnd 2: inc st in each st (16 sts).

Rnd 3: (1 sc, 1 inc st) 8 times (24 sts).

Rnd 4: 1 sc , 1 inc st; then (2 sc , 1 inc st)7 times (32 sts).

Rnd 5: (3 sc, 1 inc st) 8 times (40 sts).

Rnd 6: 2 sc, 1 inc st; (4 sc, 1 inc st) 7 times, then 2 sc (48 sts).

Rnd 7: (5 sc, 1 inc st) 8 times (56 sts).

Rnd 8: 3 sc 1 inc st; (6 sc, 1 inc st) 7 times, then 3 sc (64 sts).

Rnd 9: sc in each of 64 sts (64 sts).

Rnd 10: (7 sc, 1 inc st)8 times (72 sts).

Rnd 11: 4 sc, 1 inc st; (8 sc, 1 inc st) 7 times, then 4 sc (80 sts).

Rnd 12: sc in each of 80 sts (80 sts).

Rnd 13: (9 sc, 1 inc st) 8 times (88 sts).

Rnd 14: sc in each of 88 sts (88 sts).

Rnd 15: 5 sc, 1 inc st; (10 sc, 1 inc st) 7 times, then 5 sc (96 sts).

Rnd 16: sc in each of 96 sts (96 sts).

Rnd 17: (11 sc, 1 inc st) 8 times (104 sts).

Rnd 18: sc in each of 104 sc (104 sts).

Rnd 19: 6 sc, 1 inc st; (12 sc, 1 inc st) 7 times, then 6 sc (112 sts).

BODY

Version 1

Rnds 20–30: sc in each sc st.

Rnds 31–42: Change to CC, sc in each sc st (112 sts).

Version 2

Rnds 20-27: with MC, sc in each sc st,

Rnds 28–35 : Change CC held double, sc in each sc st.

Rnds 36–42: change to MC, sc in each st (112 sts).

BRIM

Use MC.

Versions 1 and 2

Rnd 43: (4 sc, 1 inc) 22 times, then 2 sc (134 sts).

Rnds 44-46: sc in each sc st (134 sts).

Rnd 47: (6 sc, 1 inc st) 19 times, then 1 sc (153 sts).

Rnds 48-50: sc in each sc st (153 sts).

Rnd 51: (8sc, 1 inc st) 17 times (170 sts).

Rnds 52-53: sc in each sc st (170 sts).

Version 1

Rnd 54: Crab stitch in each of the 170 sc.

Cut yarn, fasten off, and weave in ends.

Version 2

Round 54: sc in each of the 170 sc.

Round 55: (10s c, 1 inc st) 15 times, then 5 sc (180 sts).

Rounds 56–58: sc in each sc st (180 sts).

Round 59: Crab st in each of the 180 sc

Cut yarn, fasten off and weave in ends.

FINISHING

Decorate your hat with a crocheted floral motif, like the one in the linked video.

ABOUT THE DESIGNER: Lynn Murphy

I am a retired ear, nose, and throat physician living in Baton Rouge, Louisiana. Knitting for me has been a lifelong hobby producing garments inspired by color and texture.

Great Egret on Block Island

Trellis Beanie

In Fingering Yarn **2 FINE**

Designer: **Katherine Gardner**
Ravelry: **KatieKoo**

Inspired by the weatherboard architecture of the houses on Block Island and the decorative trimming on the rooftop edges, the Trellis Beanie evokes grey faded timbers and the contrasting trellis design. It is reminiscent of Spring on Block Island as the contrasting colour evokes cherry blossoms. It is a unisex design and any contrasting colour or combination of colours can be used in fingering weight yarn. High-contrast colours are recommended in order for the pattern to pop!

SIZES

XS (child), S (teen), M (women), L (men), to fit head circumference: 17 (19, 21, 23) in

HAT MEASUREMENTS

Circumference at lower edge: approx 16 (18, 20, 22) in, unstretched and unblocked.

Height, lower edge to tip: approx. 7 (8, 9, 10) in, unstretched and unblocked.

MATERIALS

Yarn

Approximately ¼ to ⅓ skein for each color of sock-weight (fingering/sport) yarn as follows. Stash-busting, leftover sock-yarn opportunities abound!

MC: Skinny Singles, from Hedgehog Fibres. Hand-dyed in Ireland, 100% merino wool, (400 m / 100 g) in Typewriter

CC: Tough Love Sock, from Sweet Georgia Yarns.

Hand-dyed in Canada, 80% superwash merino wool, 20% nylon, 388 m (425 yards) / 115 g (4 oz) in Grape Jelly

Needles

Circular needles, 3 mm, 16-in long, or size needed to achieve gauge

Four 3-mm dpns, or size to obtain given gauge.

Magic Loop technique or circular needle circumference to fit stitches comfortably (note: dpns or Magic Loop technique can be used throughout instead of circular needle, if desired)

Tools

Stitch markers: One to mark the BOR, and one for each chart pattern repeat which is 18 stitches wide repeated 7 (8, 9, 10) times depending on size (XS, S, M, L).

Post-it notes (or similar) to follow pattern line in colour charts.

Yarn needle for weaving in ends.

Bowl or balloon (inflated to desired size) to block hat after washing.

Wool wash

Scissors

GAUGE

In rib (K1, P1 two colour): 28 sts and 32 rows or rnds = 4-in square (unblocked) using 3-mm needles, or size needed to achieve gauge.

In two-colour SS chart pattern A or B, 32 sts and 36 rows or rounds = 4-in square (unblocked), using 3-mm needles, or size needed to achieve gauge.

To save time, take time to check your gauge.

NOTES

1. Hat is worked in the round following the colour charts on page 47 (Trellis Chart A and Trellis Chart B) after the initial 2-colour, K1-P1 rib. Read all rnds from right to left beginning with rnd 1 at the bottom right-hand side of chart.

2. Magic loop method can be used to knit the entire hat and facilitate the changes in stitch count. Alternatively, use a circular needle that fits the stitch count and switch to dpns when decreasing to the crown.

3. **Techniques required:** knitting in the round, decreasing, stranded colourwork.

4. When following the charts, be careful not to make the floats of yarn carried along the back of the work too tight when they are picked up again and knitted. Floats that are too tight will prevent your work from being properly blocked and may pull and distort the pattern effect. Check your tension regularly to ensure that you are leaving long-enough floats at the back and that your knitting is not being pulled in tightly!

INSTRUCTIONS

Ribbing

Using the Corrugated Rib Cast-on* (see page 47 for instructions) CO 126 (144, 162, 180) sts. (Add 1 extra st for joining in the round if desired).

Place stitch marker for the beginning of the round.

You will note that one colour is at the bottom of the stitch forming the edge and the other is the loop. Once the stitches have been cast on and joined in the round, begin K1 (MC), P1 (CC).

**Continue corrugated rib alternating colours for 12 rows (approx. 1-½ in (unblocked).

*If you find this method of casting on unfathomable, you can cast on the stitches in one colour (MC), join in the round, then join the second colour (C1) and begin the K1 (MC), P1 (C1) rib, following the instructions from the double asterisks (**).

After rib is completed, you have the option to change to a slightly larger needle if you prefer more ease in your beanie, but I prefer to stick with the same needle size (3 mm).

Main section of hat

Follow rows 1 through 18 of Trellis Chart A beginning with rnd 1 and working each rnd right to left. Repeat this pattern 7 (8, 9, 10) times, placing a stitch marker at the end of each of the 18-stitch repeats to make sure that the pattern is correct.

After Trellis Chart A is completed, knit two rows in SS using MC.

Note: This is an opportunity to consider whether you would like to make your beanie taller than the pattern measurements. If you would like to add some length here, you can insert as many rnds in SS using MC as you desire before beginning Chart B.

Begin Trellis Chart B and follow in the same manner as Trellis Chart A.

The beanie should measure approximately 5.5 in from the cast on edge to the end of Trellis Chart B (unblocked); however this may differ if you have decided to insert more MC rnds between Trellis Charts A and B.

Crown of hat

After Trellis Chart B has been completed, it is time to switch to an alternating stripe pattern and begin decreasing just before the stitch markers.

Keeping the stitch markers in place (every 18 stitches) knit in alternating colours (K1 in MC, K1 in CC) until 2 sts before the marker, and then K2tog. Repeat this decrease 6 (7, 8, 9) times across the row. 7 (8, 9, 10) stitches decreased.

Continue repeating this decrease (K to within 2 sts of marker, then K2tog), keeping the alternating striping of the colours consistent with the row below, so far as possible.

Alternate the working yarn colour for each K2tog between rows.

ABOUT THE DESIGNER: *Katherine Gardner*

Katherine's knitting mission is to keep challenging herself to improve by expanding her skills and learning new techniques to create her own designs! The Design Workshop on Block Island with Deborah Newton in May, 2023, was just what she needed to unlock the mystery of knitwear design. Since then, she has been to Shetland Wool Week for a second time, and created some new knitwear for entry into the Royal Easter Show in Sydney, Australia, where she lives. She looks forward to more workshops with Deborah Newton to further advance her skills, catch up with new friends, relax, and enjoy the natural beauty of Block Island—taking inspiration for her next knitwear designs from the Island's natural beauty and architecture.

This will create an effect where the decreases follow a spiral up to the centre of the crown at the top of the beanie, appearing in alternating colours (see photo).

FINISHING

When you have only 7(8, 9, 10) stitches remaining, take a tapestry needle, cut both yarns with a good length, thread the needle through the remaining stitches and secure tightly. Sew and weave in ends. This is a good time to attach a pompom, if desired, using these threads to secure it.

Using the yarn needle, weave in all ends on the reverse side in at least two directions before trimming. Ensure that the woven stitches do not go through to the right side.

I prefer to wet block the hat as it allows the yarn to "bloom" and it facilitates the two different yarn colour stitches to "rub shoulders" together to form a fabric. It also allows for the desired size to be achieved and the stitches to be evenly stretched out to give a smooth and finished appearance.

You can make a pompom in a colour (or colours) using left over yarn(s). Alternatively, create an icord bind-off cord or a tassel using your preferred method of choice. I have used a fake-fur pompom purchased from a yarn store but you can make your own if you prefer, or just leave it plain!

STITCH PATTERNS AND TECHNIQUES

Corrugated Rib (2-colour) Cast-on

1. Take both tails of yarn in your right hand and wrap one colour around your left thumb forming a loop with yarn crossing over itself, and wrap the other color around the your forefinger as if to do a long tail cast on.

2. Secure both threads under tension with the three remaining fingers on your left hand.

3. Hold a needle in your right hand and dip the tip of the needle underneath the left loop, up inside that loop, over the right loop, and then bring that yarn back through the left loop and onto your right needle. You have made one stitch. Repeat this step to get your required number of stitches.

View a video tutorial of the corrugated rib stitch at this link.

Trellis Chart A

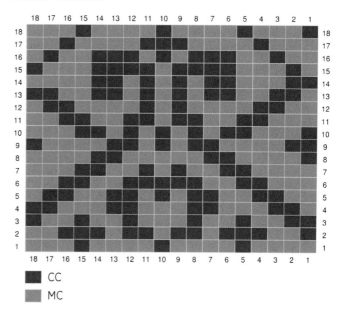

■ CC
■ MC

Trellis Chart B

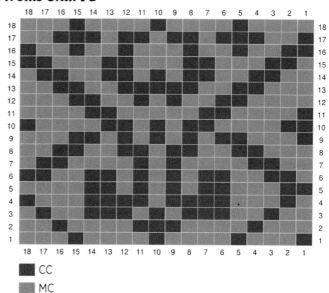

■ CC
■ MC

Verticore Hat

In Bulky Yarn 5 BULKY

Designer: **Diane Tessaglia-Hymes**
Ravelry: **diane-th**

The Verticore Hat is a warm, cozy hat with a double-thick band that combines vertical and horizontal patterns using a combination of mosaic and knit-one-below (K1B) slipped-stitch techniques. For each round, only one color of yarn is used.

The hat is worked from the bottom up, starting with a band made using the mosaic stitch and worked flat. Next, stitches are bound off to form a flap, and then the hat is joined in the round and the number of stitches reduced before knitting the body of hat and crown using the K1B stitch, which creates a brioche fabric. Decreases then shape the crown. The band is turned up and the edge tacked down or secured with a button. If desired, use a commercial or hand-crafted pompom to adorn the top of the hat.

SIZE
One size fits most (Adult)

HAT MEASUREMENTS
Circumference at lower edge: Approximately 19 in unstretched. Will fit up to 23-in head circumference.
Height, lower edge to top: 8-½ in

MATERIALS

Yarn
Approximately 60–65 g each of 2 colors of Cascade Superwash 128 (100% superwash merino wool) 128 yd (117 m)/ 100g, or Berocco Ultra Alpaca Bulky (50% Camelid Alpaca, 50% wool) 131 yd (120m)/ 100g, or any bulky-weight yarn that knits to gauge. Colors used in samples:

Pink and gray version (page 48)
MC: 875 Feather Gray Cascade 128 Superwash
CC: 515 Crystal Rose Cascade 128 Superwash

Purple and gold version (above)
MC: 72171 Berry Pie Mix Berocco Ultra Alpaca Chunky
CC: 7292 (Gold) Berocco Ultra Alpaca Chunky

Needles
U.S. Size 8 (5 mm) 24-in circular needles or 16-in straight needles (for working band flat), or size to obtain given gauge
U.S. Size 8 (5 mm) 12-in circular needles and four U. S. size 8 dpns (or your chosen way to work in the round) for body and crown of hat, or size to obtain given gauge.
Cable needle for holding stitches

Notions
1 decorative button to coordinate with yarn
Yarn needle for weaving in ends

GAUGE
Because the mosaic stitch and K1B stitches have such different gauges, please check your gauge for each stitch.
Gauge for mosaic: 17 sts = 4 in; 28 rows = 4 in. Two repeats of mosaic plus icord edging (25 sts between icords) should equal 6 in wide and 2-¼ in high.
Gauge for K1B: 12 sts = 4 in; 36 rows = 4 in. Note that

49

in K1B knitting, each visible stitch actually represents two rows.

NOTES

1. Band is worked flat, then joined in the round to complete the hat.
2. This pattern works best with two contrasting colors, or a variegated yarn and a contrasting solid yarn (see example on page 52).
3. dpns one size smaller may be used for final rows of crown decreases if you find your stitches are getting too loose.
4. Placing markers at the beginning of each mosaic pattern repeat can help you stay on track.

INSTRUCTIONS

Band

Using MC, CO 91 st using long-tail cast on. Leave a tail about 8-in long for tacking down the band and weaving in later.

The band is created using in the mosaic stitch, worked from the Verticore Mosaic Chart or written instructions on page 52. The section marked by a red square in the chart is knitted 7 times per row.

   Knit each row in the chart two times (12 rows) and then knit the chart again one more time (24 total rows knitted), paying particular attention to whether the yarn is slipped at the end of each row to the front or to the back, and whether the first three stitches are knitted or purled.

This mosaic stitch instructional video on YouTube provides a good demonstration of the mosaic stitch.

Transition
Cut CC, leaving a 6-inch tail to weave in later.

Transition Row 1:

- Put first st on cable holder and hold to back. Using MC, K1 from needle then return the st that is on the cable needle back to the left needle. K2tog.
- Bind off first st on right needle, then bind off 9 more sts.
- P to 3 sts before end.
- Sl next 2 sts to cable needle and hold to front.
- K2tog using 1 st from cable needle and 1 st from left needle.
- K final st from cable needle. 79 sts on needle.

Transition Row 2: Using 12-in circular needle, K1, (K1, K2tog) 24 times. K to end. (54 sts on needle)

Transition Row 3: PM, join to knit in round and K 1 round. SM.

Body of Hat

The body of the hat alternates yarn color every row and uses the K1B "column stitch" to create vertical stripes. To learn more about K1B, check out Elise Duvekot's book or her patterns in Ravelry.

   Purl Soho provides a video of how to make the K1B stitch. Note that in this video, the stitch between the K1B stitches is purled (not knitted as in the Verticore Hat), and the example uses only one color of yarn.

Body Rnd 1: Using CC (join on first row), (K1, K1B) 27 times to EOR, SM.

Body Rnd 2: Using color MC, (K1B, K1) 27 times to EOR, SM.

Work these two rows for 7 in or desired length (approximately 64 rows, or 32 counted row stitches) in K1B stitch, alternating colors and slipping the marker as you come to it. After the second round, you will always K1B into the column of stitches that

---

ABOUT THE DESIGNER: Diane Tessaglia-Hymes

Diane is a communications specialist and freelance graphic designer who first learned to knit when she was 16 years old but has been avidly knitting for the past 15 years. She recently ventured into designing knitted garments, drawing inspiration from science and the natural world, with a fascination for color, light, and the patterns created by reflection and shadow. She strives for designs that are functional yet beautiful, that achieve a balance between challenging the knitter and allowing time for meditative repetition, and that have unusual yet efficient construction. When not knitting or working, she enjoys cooking, sewing, managing her Airbnb, and spending time with family. She lives in upstate New York with her husband and three cats.

matches the working yarn color. End with a round using MC.

Crown Decreases

Use [right-leaning, knit-one-below double decreases](#) (RLDD) from linked video or instructions at right.

Switch to dpns for the crown decreases, or when stitches on needle become too spread out.

Crown Rnd 1 (decrease rnd): Using CC,
[K1, K1B] 3 times, K1, RLDD, PM,
[K1, K1B] 4 times, K1, RLDD, PM,
[K1, K1B] 3 times, K1, RLDD, PM,
[K1, K1B] 4 times, K1, RLDD, PM,
[K1, K1B] 3 times, K1, RLDD, PM (44 sts on needles)

Crown Rnd 2: Using MC, (K1B, K1) all around, slipping markers as you come to them.

Crown Rnd 3: Using CC, (K1, K1B) all around, slipping markers as you come to them.

Crown Rnd 4: Repeat Crown Rnd 2

Above: Close-up of RLDD
Below: Close-up of transition rows and WS of split band.

Crown Rnd 5 (decrease rnd): Using CC
[K1, K1B] 2 times, K1, RLDD, SM,
[K1, K1B] 3 times, K1. RLDD, SM,
[K1, K1B] 2 times, K1, RLDD, SM,
[K1, K1B] 3 times, K1, RLDD, SM,
[K1, K1B] 2 times, K1, RLDD. SM (34 sts on needles)

Crown Rnds 6–8: Repeat Crown Rnds 2–4.

Crown Rnd 9 (decrease rnd): Using CC,
K1, K1B, K1, RLDD, SM,
[K1, K1B] 2 times, K1, RLDD, SM,
K1, K1B, K1, RLDD, SM,
[K1, K1B] 2 times, K1, RLDD, SM,
K1, K1B, K1, RLDD, SM (24 sts on needles)

Crown Rnds 10–12: Repeat Crown Rnds 2–4.

Crown Rnd 13 (decrease rnd): Using CC,
K1, RLDD, SM,
K1, K1B, K1, RLDD, SM,
K1, RLDD, SM,
K1, K1B, K1, RLDD, SM,
K1, RLDD, SM. (14 sts on needles)

Crown Rnds 14–16: Repeat Crown Rnds 2–4.

Cut yarn leaving a 10-in tail. Thread tapestry needle and slide it through stitches on needle(s) as you remove them. Tighten, bring yarn to wrong side of hat, and fasten.

FINISHING

- Weave in all ends, and tack down flap to hold it and then sew on a button or other decoration.
- Blocking not needed.
- Add a pompom to the top, using a commercial one, or make one from left-over yarn.
- To make it easy to remove the pompom for washing, sew one side of a ½-in snap to the hat and sew or hot-glue the other side of the snap to the pompom.

STITCH PATTERN AND TECHNIQUES

RLDD—Right-leaning K1B double decrease

- S1B knitwise (Slip 1 below): Insert needle as if to knit into stitch directly below first stitch on left-hand needle.
- K1, and then pass the two loops from S1B over stitch just knitted
- Prepare for next stitch: S1B purlwise, and return both sts of S1B to left needle without twisting
- Slip stitch on right needle to left needle, and pass the two loops of S1B over stitch just slipped
- Return stitch to right needle, slipping it purlwise.

Written instructions for Verticore Mosaic Chart

Setup Row: Using MC, sl 3 wyif, K to 3 sts before the end, sl 3 wyif

Read odd rows from right to left and even rows from left to right. This section is knit flat.

Row 1 (RS): K3 with MC. Join CC first time, and K1, [sl2 wyib, K7, sl2 wyib, K1] 7 times, sl3 wyib

Row 2 (WS): Still using CC, P3. Bring yarn to back and [K1, sl2 wyib, K7, sl2 wyib] 7 times, K1, sl3wyif.

Row 3 (RS): K3 with CC. Pick up MC and K1 [K3, sl2 wyib, K1, sl2 wyib K4] 7 times, sl3 wyib.

Row 4 (WS): Still using MC, P3. Bring yarn to back and [K4, sl2 wyif, K1, sl2 wyif, K3] 7 times, K1, sl3 wyif.

Row 5 (RS): Using MC, K3. Change to CC and K85, sl3 wyib.

Row 6 (WS): Still using CC, P3. Bring yarn to back and K85, sl3 wyif.

Row 7 (RS): K3 with CC. Pick up MC and K1, [sl2 wyib, K7, sl2 wyib, K1] 7 times, sl3 wyib.

Row 8 (WS): Still using MC, P3. Bring yarn to back and [K1, sl2 wyib, K7, sl2 wyib] 7 times, K1, sl3wyif.

Row 9 (RS): K3 with MC. Pick up CC and K1, [K3, sl2 wyib, K1, sl2 wyib, K4] 7 times, sl3 wyib.

Row 10 (WS): Still using CC, P3. Bring yarn to back and [K4, sl2 wyif, K1, sl2 wyif, K3] 7 times, K1, sl3 wyif.

Row 11 (RS): Using MC, K3. Pick up CC and K85, sl3 wyib.

Row 12 (WS): Still using CC, P3, K85, sl3 wyif.

Row 13-24: Repeat Rows 1 to 12 one more time.

Sample above was knit in Ella Rae Chunky Merino Lace in colors 502—Red Rose Brown and 523—Olive Fuchsia Brown (discontinued yarn).

Verticore Mosaic Chart

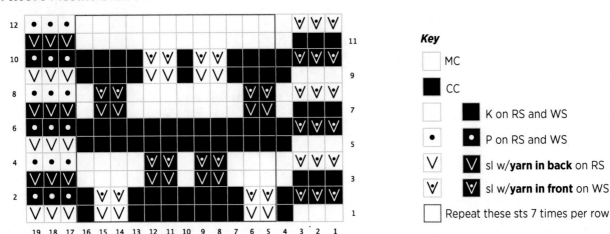

Key

☐ MC		
■ CC		
☐	■	K on RS and WS
•	⊡	P on RS and WS
V	V	sl w/**yarn in back** on RS
V̇	V̇	sl w/**yarn in front** on WS
☐		Repeat these sts 7 times per row

NOTE: This chart includes a knitted-on i-cord on each side. When working from the chart, remember that all rows in the chart are knitted, except for the icord on the left side, which is purled on the WS. Change colors after working the first three sts (the icord) of each RS (odd-numbered) row. The section marked by a red square in the chart is knitted 7 times per row.

Rows 1, 2, 5, 6, 9 an 10 are knit with CC (the darker of your two colors) and rows 3, 4, 7, 8, 11, and 12 are knit with MC (the lighter of your two colors). On each row, stitches marked with V or V̇ are slipped. *Make sure these stitches are always slipped with yarn brought to the WS.*

Southeast Lighthouse on Block Island.

Deb releases a Palm Warbler that has just been banded, while Teema captures the moment.

The designers' local yarn stores

	Address	Contact information	Local to...
Australia			
	Skein Sisters 721 New Canterbury Road Dulwich Hill NSW 2203 Australia	www.skeinsisters.com.au	Katherine Gardner
USA			
Maine	The Yarn Sellar 891 US Rte 1 York ME 03909	207 351-1987	Lauren Altieri
Maryland	Lovely Yarns 3610 Falls Road Hampden MD 21211	410 662-9276 Lovelyyarns.com	Kitty Savel
Massachusetts	Plymouth Harbor Knits 170 Water St Plymouth , MA 02360	Plymouthharborknits.com 774 283-4704	Jennifer Curly Girl
	A Garden for Knitters The Hayscales Building, 2 Johnson St. Suite 3, North Andover, MA	978-682-3297 agardenforknitters.com jacqui@agardenforknitters.com	Brenda Hyland-Miller
Montana	Stix 821 W Mendenhall St Bozeman, MT 59715	406-556-5786 Stixyarn.com	Teema Loeffelholz
New Hampshire	Hodgepodge Yarns and Fibers 59 Belknap Ave. Newport, NH 03773	+1 603-863-1470	Maureen Cullen
New York	Homespun Boutique 51 East Main Street Trumansburg, NY, 14886	(607) 387-7786 (cash or check only) www.facebook.com/ homespunithaca/	Diane Tessaglia-Hymes
	Fiber Arts in the Glen 315 N. Franklin Street Watkins Glen, NY 14891	607-535-9710 fiberartsintheglen.com fiberartsintheglen@gmail.com	Diane Tessaglia-Hymes
Washington	Hazel Knits 2000 Airport Way S #1 Seattle, WA 98134 206 250-1312	Hazelknits.com Owner: Wendee Shulsen	Barbara Hyland-Hill Brenda Hyland-Miller
Online			
	Knit Picks	Knitpicks.com	Deb Frazier
	WEBS, America's Yarn Store 75 Service Center Rd Northampton, MA 01060	yarn.com	Lynn Murphy

Sunset from the 1661 Inn

Made in the USA
Coppell, TX
01 August 2024

35472486R00036